Telescope

Sandy Florian

Action Books
Notre Dame, Indiana
2006

Action Books
Joyelle McSweeney and Johannes Göransson, Editors
Jesper Göransson, Art Director
Kristina Sigler, Assistant Editor
John Dermot Woods, Web Design
Kwoya Fagin, 2005-2006 Editorial Intern

Action Books gratefully acknowledges the instrumental support of the
University of Notre Dame.

Action Books
Department of English
University of Notre Dame
356 O'Shaughnessy Hall
Notre Dame, IN 46556-5639

Learn more about us at www.actionbooks.org.

Contents

A board. A slab. A draught. A frame strewn with sand for the delineation of figures. A sandbox. And. Geometrical diagrams. Or. A frame divided in two sections and in which round wooden plums slide upon parallel rods. For performing the functions of arithmetic. Finding mechanical solutions to mathematical problems. Addition and subtraction. Multiplication and division. Both square and cube root operations. On numbers. As. A set of positive integers unique in meaning and fixed in order. But. If the value of the plum changes according to its position on the rod, you find that I am divisible. Can be rendered invisible. That I can be reduced, diminished, and deducted from the larger quantities. I am trying to discover the value of me. But. I am dumb to the wonders of your great numbers.

A child puts a penny in a penny loafer. A woman with two broken fingers carries three bags up four stairs. Five or six men stamp their feet in the snow. And. In the middle of a rectangular room, halfway across the world, seven empty chairs form a circle. For. A nine inch statue portrays a man on the back of an ox. And. I am trying to accrue. I am trying to accumulate. But. You have given me the gift of two glass eyes. Or. You've added eight and subtracted ten.

The word is derived from a Semitic word *ibeq*. To wipe the dust. And. In architecture, a slab on the top of the capital of a column. In the Ionic orders, a square flat plate. In the Corinthian and Composite, variously cut and ornamented. See. You are bedazzled. You stand at the edge of a hundred horizons wearing a thousand crowns. While I, in this world, am slowly disappearing. As is this image of you. For. Any number times zero. Always equals zero.

Balloon

A blown globe of double leather struck high and low by an arm defended by a bracer of wood. And. The game played with such a globe. Or. A ball of pasteboard stuffed with combustible matter which, when fired from a mortar, mounts to the sky then bursts into the brighter stars. A *rondure* placed on a pillar to crown it. As. A circular or gracefully rounded object. Or. An airtight envelope of pear-shaped silk which, when inflated with the lighter gasses, rises high into the air. To large balloons, a basket strong enough to carry human beings is attached. For use for. Observation of atmospheric disturbance. Military reconnoitering. And. As a means for wandering toward the moon. For. If this ship can skip you from the earth to the stars whenever your windy blows do bound, I choose to harness this helium. I confine it in a varnished silk and depend on the principles of buoyant force. For. According to Archimedes, a body submerged is buoyed by a force equal to the weight of the fluid displaced by the body. Or. If b represents buoyancy and w the weight of the displaced, I eat the experimental gum. I turn blue and inflate like a giant balloon. While you. Floating in your own ship. Make rounded shadows on the greener grounds.

A goblet with two short necks used to receive products of a distillation. As. Interpose a large glass between retort and recipient. Or. Let me pass through your glass balloon. I see through this glass so darkly. And. I suffer from another synovial inflammation. For. The stars are darkled by your opaque orb.

On the other hand, a colloquial term used for any event. As when I ask, "What time does the balloon go up?" you understand, "When is the parade of your home coming home?" and reply so dryly, "Merely because I gave you a beery kiss in the bar, you can't believe the whole balloon's going up."

Anything inflated, empty, and hollow. As. A batsman who has failed to win points gets a blob, a balloon, a goose. The container for words in comic engravings, as issued from the mouths of cartoon people. Otherwise. From their heads. As. Diabolical sentiments were represented as issuing from his head in fat balloons. But. If b represents buoyancy, and you are struck with such wanderlust, I am all blown up like a penny balloon. And. My hands feel just like two balloons. For. I am once again struck by the same solid ceiling. In another ballroom ball.

Clock

Water dripping through a hole in a jar. Or. Sand dripping through two hollows coned together. The downy head of a dandelion in seed. Or. The core of an apple. As. Take an apple and peal him, and cut out the clocks thereof. But. If the spin of the globe is used as a counter, you draw twelve numbers on the rounded face and depress a pin. You look to the sky and articulate the hour. Then. Wind it up and hear how it hums. While I, wandering through the Museum of My Body Parts, ask you to tell me the story of time.

You say, See here. In plain sight are the weights which furnish the power. The pendulum which regulates speed. Up and behind is a Chinese puzzle of wheels. The pendulum is hung by a thin spring of steal. The cord from which the weight hangs is wrapped around the barrel. Like the rope on the windlass of a boat at sea. Push the pendulum and the pulse wakes up. Like the palace in the story of Sleeping Beauty. But. If the globe now spins more slowly than it did a million years ago, I don't know this fairy and ask you to tell me the tale.

A muzzled dog, chained, runs circles around a rabid tree in the tropics. Thus, although we cannot live, we are bothered by talking.

You say, Measurement. I say, Certainly. But I have my doubts. First, this pendulum falls to sleep with the same disease of dreams. Rigor mortis settles on my hands the same way cold settles on a lake. Or. The hands of the clock. Joints lock and the muscles contract. Language is made law by the man in cloak. And, yes, I know the globe still spins, but this grandfather of gravity has no face at all.

For ordinary purposes, the face of the sun and moon. Or. The shadows of the tree. The position of the stars at night. In prose, you say, To discover the state of things. Or. A scheme in bombing. But when I ask you to tell me the story of time and why the clock strikes no more, you say that you cannot remember ever asking me to dance.

A handheld musical instrument invented by Damian in Vienna. Consisting of. Folded bellows to which a button board is attached. Depressed buttons open the valves and admit wind over the reeds. Those narrow tongues of metal. Some are riveted to the upper board. Some to the lower. Or. A keyboard accordion. The piano kind of ivory keys made from the tusks of African elephants. And. If the pitch of the note depends on the length of the reeds, your right hand holds the Palace. While your left manipulates the Prison. With skill you make a melancholy music in the middle. And. Three bass keys of the tonic and dominant chords. You must see that I, too, am trying to play at your toy. But. I am all thumbs. Fumbling. For. This time it is I who suffer from the strange numbness. Born from the adagio of your decrescendo.

From *accordare*. As. To tune an instrument. Or. To play in unison. The termination of the word imitates the clarion. As. A shrill sounding trumpet with a narrow tube used as a signal in war. And. The sound of war. The crowing of cocks. Or. Carrion. As. Corpse or carcass. For. This flesh unfit for food. And. They're playing our song.

The frame and tongue are one, as is the case with Jew's harps. And. The reeds are mounted on sideboard, as is the case with concertinas. Having a series of folds. As. The lenses on cameras. But. If each button sounds two different notes, one upon the inhalation, the other upon the exhalation, you take your show to Vaudeville. Between Palace and Prison, you keep your time in tune. A door, skirt, wall, or window. While I. See. I am becoming the handless widow of your accordion window. For. This is the middle without center.

Van Guericke's little weather man. Or. A tube of brass and glass dipped in a basin of water. Or. Mercury. Which rises higher in fairer weather and falls within the storm. The work of muttering magicians. Or. An instrument for measuring atmospheric pressure. As. The aneroid barometer. As. A portable device that measures pressure not by the heights of Mercury but by its action on the lid. Of. The hermetically sealed box. But. If the pocket aneroid resembles a watch in its appearance, you strap the barometer onto your wrist. Strap my body on to yours. Leap out from the skywriting plane. And. Fall. For.

Take a tube a yard long, close it at one end and fill it with Mercury. God of travel and of thievery. Close the tube at one end and invert it in a vessel. You will soon see that very few drops will drop out. As. The atmosphere pressing upon the surface supports the weight of the Mercury. And. If there is a difference between the atmosphere. And. The apocalypse of your falling body. I ask you to stop pressing yourself upon.

There you see the city of rain. There, the pink structures of its politic. Here. My widening wound. Or. My wide remorse for time. For. Hallowed be thy name. Your barometer. Six. Five. Four. Is falling. For. If the pocket aneroid resembles a watch in its appearance, glycerine can used in place of Mercury for exacter readings. As. Sweet syrupy fluid obtained from fats by. Saponification. And. You must now see. We are running out of time. For. The barometer was first made public by the nobler searchers of nature. And. Your fob. Like a barometer. Shows the temper of your beating heart. As. An indicator of fluctuations. Or. A standard for comparison. Both the benchmark and the touchstone. The yardstick and the paradigm. Are we diving? Or am I dying? For. This time, the child just dreams. Of parachutes. In bloom.

A floating needle on a cork in water. Or. A needle suspended by its middle point. Or. I sail the seas exploring the improvisation of your geography. Not exactly. But. If the globe is 7000 miles in diameter, you stand, the mariner on the mountain, miles high. You draw a circle on the ground and pivot on your peak. In the center, you choose West and adjust your gaze. The orbs of your eyes reflect the vibration damp in the distant horizon. I adjust my imprecise instrument and wonder which way you're headed.

If the globe is 7000 miles in diameter, I attach you to the surface of that which comes to pass, losing you through the space between my fingers. A child stands in a sandbox. Or. An hourglass. Empty? While I choose to rest quickly in the soft nook of your elbow. Hello elbow. Lend me your bowl and fill it with synovial fluid. I am trying hard not to tip this ship.

In the improved form, I sail the seas by day and by night. My direction needs correction. Or. A complicated calculation. Skirting shores by the hours and, yes, I know about the stars, but I would never strike brazenly in this splinter of wood.

If the globe is 7000 miles in diameter, dogs run circles around you in your rough terrain. I sail this hollow bowl, steered not by deviation. But. By the logic of a flower. Or. A saw for cutting curves of a mediocre size. A signal from a mountain peak. A window. Not wide.

A needle swings over the disk divided by minutes and seconds. By sight and by screw, I calculate. You walk, legs long, in your own gazing direction, rendering me inconceivable in my domain. You move, yes, but I need order. Within the bounds of moderation. For I am among the Things That Decay. I am running out of compass. Or. Out of compassion. To speak is to speak within limits. An artful device.

A bound book of heavenly bodies. Or. A volume of verification. Illustrative plates and large engravings. As. The Italian. Assembled To Order. The conspectus of a subject arranged in tables. And. A folio. A reference. Diagrams delineating both geopolitics and topography. A satellite of Saturn. And. One who sustains a greater burden. A supporter. A mainstay. As. The Uppermost vertebra which supports the skull. Articulated above with the occipital. As. Ring of bone. Without body. Made of arches and of process. For. To prop. To carry. To bear. A silky type of satin. As. The fat lady in a tawdry atlas. Of gaudy Gold and purple. But. If the first book was constructed from Ptolemy's calculations, you call yourself the fathomer of fathoms. Keeper of tall pillars. You call yourself both the philosopher and the astronomer. But. These maps are all outdated. Or. You failed to take into account for Portuguese and Spanish discoveries. The west-east orientation of Scotland. And. I bear the world upon my shoulders. The bodies of half-men used as columns.

Atlas of anatomy. Atlas of ethnography. Chromosomic compositions. And. A chart. Delineation. Or. Design. A large drawing paper. And. A beetle. As. Olive-green lamellicorn found in the East.

Twenty bound maps. Twenty seven. Or. The first book was constructed from Ptolemy's calculations. Thirty eight and a publisher in Rome. Fifty three that cover the countries. These are the descriptions of Universe. As. The son of Asia. Punished by Zeus. For. A mixture of formats. Lacking vision. So, you commission a set that could be more easily consulted. Are credited for the conversion in the history of cartography. As. The drawing of doodles. Circlets denote cities. Dots denote towns. But. Whatever the truth, to support. To prop. To carry. I make myself sustainer of your estate. Or. I am atlasing a coop of forty fowls unfeathered.

The loci of the unnamed world and the wandering world of hell. Or. A vaulted church shut down beneath the earth. A subterranean receptacle for the dead. Or. The crisscrossed graves of honey. As. The necropolis under the Basilica. On Appian Way, near Rome. At the Alyscamps in Arles. But. The evidence here doesn't settle the dispute. So. Bury the king's corpse. Or. Bury the king's conscience. But. When you have washed my body, throw the birds in the pit. For. This is a word of mongrel composition. Half Greek. Half Latin. Signifying as much as near to. Then, ten miles round. As. Death is unclean. Under the cornfields. Under the guns. But. If the abandoned catacombs could with such ease be so forgotten, you forget that I am the handmaiden of your hearth. The handmaiden of your heartbreak. And. You win this upper world with your peripatetic walls. While my gates can only widen. For. Mine the gates of Hades. This is the grotto.

Subterranean Rome. Necropolis built by piety. Or. Unrequited love. For the corpse in stale decay.

The hollow of a drinking vessel. A cup, or bowl, or boat. A handbag or a knapsack. An underground escape. A tunnel of mummies. Some bodies are better preserved. Some are set to poses. As. Two children together in a rocking chair. Or. The sight of funeral feasts and frolic. In Paris, the site for sewage, and for skulls. In modern times, a compartment for storing wine. As. The blood of Christ. The sap from the fruit-bearing tree. But. If the abandoned catacombs could with such ease be so forgotten, I must with word remind you. While the air above waxes still, I am suffering your interment. I am perishing from your forgetting. For. Remembrance is a life of grief. And. I reside in the grace of your grave eye. Or. The apple.

A blockade on a watercourse. The piece of water thus impounded. Or. The flat land that is drained. And. A stop of earth and twigs. A causeway through the bogs. A partition, a repression, a plug. As. A valve forever closed. Or. A pond for watering cattle. But. If God's work is the work of beavers, you calculate with care the force of pressure. Then. Flood the hollows of high tunnels. Harness its hydraulics. And. Furnish your metropolis with the unnatural application. While I, subject to the half-shadows of your highness, build these castles made of sand. Or. These castles made of sound. For. This time, it is I who put my ear to the waterlogged wall and listen. It is my willy-nilly will to rest. In the vestibules of your ventricles.

The Lord as prefix. And. The opprobrious name given to Our Mother. As. Let the Devil and his dam haunt you. And. He worries the worst. That she is the Devil's dam. To stop. To block. To shut. Confine. But. If God's work is the work of beavers, you dam all the doors. Like a ridge of mountains dams the cloud. And. While you use your finger to plug the leak, I fail to worry the wall. In the sleepy pool above the dam. The Pool beneath that never stills.

An Indian coin the value of a quarter rupee. Or. Single pieces in a game of checkers. This is the backwards mad. Or. This is the flax dam festering in townland. Both to birth and to occlude. As. Opening. Closing. Opening. Closing. The industry augurs well for the formation. Or. That's water over the dam. Water under the bridge. I put the penny in the penny loafer and sing. For. Unlike skeletal muscles, the heart works on the all or nothing law.

The drum that oscillates water from laundry. Or. The outward pull of a ball on a string. Newton's first law of motion, certainly. And. The curved contraption in which humans are enclosed. For reasons of experimentation. For. If you can filter the astronaut from the man, or the dervish from the Devil, you whirl this bucket round your head in the clockwise direction. Compass-wise? Never. You risk separating the *me* from *it*. In the periphery of your central axis. While you twirl your bucket round. North and south. With skill, you chance not to spill my ship. But. This boat is capsized and the oars are lost. And. This time, it is I who want to communicate. But. Because you remain nameless, I call this Conundrum a Catastrophe and attempt to measure the speed of things that fly out.

There is a general appreciation that the force can be grown by swelling the speed of the rotation. The mass of the object. Or. The radius of the circle. But perhaps not so generally appreciated is the fact. Whereas force is proportional, cold courage cannot be constrained. This time, the child, face flat against the rubberized curve, watches the floor drop from under his feet. This time, it is I who am scared into stiffness. For, if the difference between the things that stay and the things that fly away be restraint, I struggle to dismount the horse from the merry-go-round and go.

The rotor that throws cream from milk. And. The mechanism that measures sedimentation rates. Of. Inflammations in the body rigid. For. If you can filter the astronaut from the man, you can use the same device to clarify vaccines. And. To purify both milk and motor oil. Reactor grade uranium. You separate those bodies of different specific gravities and call the gods mercurial. As. Points become lines and drop. But This time, it is I who want to beg of you. Stop testing my toleration to acceleration. For. This time it is I who fail to measure the time falling bodies take to light.

An ascending chamber used for raising bodies high in buildings. Or. A platform raised in a vertical passage to transport people and their freight. A surface attached to a stabilizer for the production of. Upward motions. Or. A bucket attached to a conveyor for hoisting. A granary equipped with devices for discharging. A surgical instrument used to raise sunken parts. Like fragments of bone. Or. For separating contiguous parts. But. If this chamber can ascend you to the highest heavens, I insist that I am sinking. Or. That I am stuck. Sick like any seasick sailor. For. This elevator is spinning. Or. This elevator has come loose in its shaft. And. I have this dream where we are listening to elevator music. And. You cover my mouth with tape. For. A dental instrument for the removal of teeth. Or. The part of tooth that can't be gripped.

Two elevators. A crowd of ten mounts the left. There's no room for me and my tree. The door to the right. And. You are on the elevator. I struggle. It's me and my tree. But. You push a button with scalloped edges. White button the color of pearl. And. There's someone crying on the loudspeaker.

A muscle which raises limb or bone. As. The tendinous flesh that opens the jaw. Or. One of the two flat joints of the maxillary feelers. As. In hive or humble, the elevator has not two but four joints. For. Cables with a cabin at one end and counterweights at the other. Pass first over the driver, then over the idler, and back over the driver. For. A motor in either direction. Operated by levers. What would happen if the cabin should fall? Watch the powerful steel jaws of the cabin clamping. Like the elevator flesh that clamps my wrists.

A furniture of firebrick used for metallurgical operations. Or. A chamber of incendiaries for subjection to the fixed attributes of heat. The fire of a volcano. Or. The volcano itself. As. A conical mountain that communicates by crater with the interior of the globe. Or. Its inferior. But. If the modern oven can achieve the temperature of 7000 degrees, you use the crematorium for the burning of the birds. Or. The burning of my body. For. By smelting or with sword, you render me Combustible among the Things To Be Destroyed.

If the modern oven can achieve the temperature of 7000 degrees, I arrange the logs of my limbs in this chimney of stars. For. The lameness of Vulcan and the infidelity of Venus are the occasional subject of literary allusions. And. By heart or by hearth, I become petrified by the pear-shaped presence of your absence.

A womb. A boiler. A crucible. Or. A tyrannical test or trial. An incinerator of sins. And. The fireplace of a marine boiler. For. I am trying hard to control this corrosion. But. Because of the doctrines of paterfamilias, I seek the child behind every corner. Find only broadness of bedrock.

With drift, a passage leading into an upcast pit. With feeder, one who stokes the embers. With filler, one who remains at the top and empties the loaded barrows. With cadmia, the oxide of zinc that collects in the flues of furnaces smelting. Zinciferous ores. But. If the modern oven can achieve the temperature of 7000 degrees, I am bewildered by your pyromania For. If the furnace has the virtue to disintegrate atoms, it also has the virtue of converting this lump of Dark Dust and Sand into a body as clear as Crystal. For. With glow, the Eastern resumption.

A foundry for traders conducting business in foreign countries. Or. A merchant company's trading station. The body of factors in any one place. Employment, office, or position of a factor. As. A doer. An agent. One who does. Things. And. To the intent he might remain in the factory with the factor. Or. A building with a plant for the machine-making of goods. Exactly. But. If the starting point of modern industry is the instrument of mechanical production, reproduction, you are in the practice of accumulation and I am in the practice of commodifying myself. I am striving for Thinghood. For. To be sensuous is to suffer. And. Your machine is accommodating itself to the weakness of my stiff body in order to make me a tooth of its wide system. Or. My unbeing. Factory of river. Factory of rain. Link in the Alps' globe-girding chain.

A prison. A police station. A whorehouse. As. The lass I adore, the lass for me, is the lass in the female factory. But. This factory of manifold machines is a perpetuum mobile. These machines could produce forever. And. If the machines are in the production of your sense of forever, the magnitude of this great profit whets your appetite for more time. You endeavor to thoroughly exploit the sunny times of your first love by prolonging the unfixed day. The child, now five, works hours fifteen. While I. Under the burden of this rock, suffer its forever falling backwards. I am rheumatic. Paralytic. I am become stillborn.

A graveyard. A cemetery. A nuclear reactor. A concentration camp where prisoners are systematically murdered. For. If the starting point of modern industry is the revolution of the instruments, this revolution attains its most developed form in the organized system of. I have become your factory hand, the automaton, feeder of your unmitigated requirements. And. A skyline park emitting cyclone clouds of your sweet smoke.

Cognizable action in general. And. Doubtless deed as opposed to language. Thing done. Thing performed. In a neutral sense, a course of conduct. As. At length you commit a fact that accomplishes my annihilation. And. Tenacious in fact if not in word. Or. Having an effect in law. As. If the tenant discontinues, descends, or does any fact whatsoever. Exactly. The creation, assertion, or accomplishment of things. As. All effects wrought by fact are produced by authentic testimony. And. If the fact can be positively apprehended, you seek only capital truth. Calculable logic. Austere evidence that proves the unequivocal event. I, on the other hand, can hear only music. For. I am among the Things That Dream. Moved only by. Things That Press On My Heart.

Most definitely, a brave and benevolent exploit. A *feat*, from which the word is unquestionably derived. Of valor and of skill. As. Your facts of war and facts of blood all excel in fact of arms. Contrarily, an evil deed or crime. Actual guilt as opposed to suspicion. As. If Great Julius could not rest satisfied that his wife was free from fact. Mathematically, the product of two or more factors multiplied together. As. The third quantity here is called Product. Fact. Rectangle. Occasionally, with an exclamation mark, used as emphatic assertion of the accuracy of a statement.

Something has happened. Fact! Something has actually occurred. Fact! Reality can be known and its data can be collected. For. You are the attorney of truth. The fact is. You stand on Buckingham. You walk across London Bridge. I, on the other hand, live in the world of windmills. And. I ask you to stop disproving my fictions. See. While you commit yourself to the harder science, I am truth-terrified. I skill myself instead the art of unmaking. For. To undo the deeds that have undone these dreams. Is the noblest of all metaphors.

A cannon mounted on a carriage and from which missiles are cast by the force of powder. Or. A metal pipe from which shots are fired at high velocities. Any portable firearm. As. A musket or a fowling piece. A rifle or a revolver. See the pistol lying in the periphery of the prison. For. A long single barreled gun is called a goose-gun. A piece of ordnance is called a great gun. One mechanically loaded and fired is called a machine gun. As. The mechanical wonder of World War I. Give high flying men the power to fire ten shots per second. Through the spinning propellers of airplanes. But. If the a difference between the morning and evening guns lies in the ticking of clocks, the word was used in England for an Engine long before the powder was found out. Black blend of nitrate, charcoal, and sulfur. But. If the difference between the morning and the evening guns lies in the ticking of clocks, you sling your gun over your right shoulder. Call yourself a winter hunter and wander under the covered sun. For. You have as many guns as there are birds in the sky. And. I am fumbling toward these geese in tumble. Or. I am listening to the postman's steady *rat-a-tat-tat*. For. My damaged elbow prevents me from sleeping until the morning ghosts and their guns. Or. I am now asleep in your machine-gun dreams.

Because. This is the season for hunting geese. And. It being represented that the evening gun might discover us, you were prevailed upon to omit. For. To be sure as a gun is to be dead certain. To stick to one's guns is to be rigidly fixed. To carry the guns is to have capacity for power. And. To be under the gun is to be hurried. But. To measure the weight of guns and butter is to determine the need for military expansion. At the expense of socioeconomic developments. For. The government cannot run from their guns. And. This is the start of another race. Or. Another world war. For. This is nothing but a six-shooter suicide. One of many instances of bestowing female names on the engines of war. Thus. A hypodermic needle used by heroin addicts.

A road over a river. An avenue over a ravine. A plank that goes from bank to bank. Or. A structure of architectural elaboration. Affording higher passageway between two points. As. Faith builds a bridge. Supported by arch, pier, and chain. From this world to the heavens. Or. By girder and tube. From my world to you. As. Rocks across a ground. A gangway between two hatchways. A road supported by boats moored abreast across a stream. For. A fallen tree over a stream. And. If to burn the bridge behind you is to burn your own boat, the word bride is in your bridge. This world is not mine. Or. I am not in it. For. A portion of the brain which curves between the two lobes of the cerebellum in front of the medulla oblongata. A platform suspended in the front of a canvas. Upright wood over which strings are stretched. And. Which transmits their vibrations to the. This is my body blank. For. If the strings of the violin resemble double pendulums, a plankway by which ore is conveyed to the mouth of the smelting furnace. You are the keeper of doubles and trebles. From cape to cape with bridge-like shape, over the torrent sea.

Bridge tone. Bridge tree. Splinter bar of the swingle tree. A floating jetty out to sea. The adjustable beam that supports a stone. Rhythmic constructions. Of your introductions. Crown, bar, and bond. A tripod for holding pots over flames. In billiards, a cross-shaped rose. In saddlery, a tongueless buckle. In dentistry, falsity of tooth. To shorten. To lessen. To curtail. As. None but the Lord can bridge my days. And. I am trying hard to bridge the distance between us. Gestures bridge my way to spoken language. But I am as *beside the bridge*. Off track. I've gone astray. An attractive way of escape. These are the Gates of Hell. For. You have laid the bridge of silver for me, your flying enemy.

The town of starry tents that travels static roads. Or. The parking lot that blossoms overnight. And. The blare of the calliope. The bark of the bagman. Or. You stand heavenly over heathens in search of wide horizons. Or. The leaf of the heliotrope. But. If the time devoted entirely to pleasure intervenes between Boxing Day and Ash Wednesday, you bring the same symmetry of that old clock and compass to the nose of the clown. Or. To the coin you twist between your fingers. You toss your dazzling dime onto your lucky number and watch the whirl of the wheel of chance. While I, dressed in my sideshow sequins, tip my top hat to show. It is the season of the unadorned rabbit.

If the time devoted entirely to pleasure intervenes between the box and its ashes, the history of the word is illustrated by the parallel name *Carnem Laxare*. See. This history is hung without a witness. For. As you watch without distraction your whirling world, the magician flashes the saw and the box. While I, bidding farewell to my flesh, wave goodbye from the stage with my stiff unfisted hands.

In France, it comprises of *Jeudi gras*, *Dimanche gras*, *Lundi gras*, and *Mardi gras*. Elsewhere, the carnival of my sweet love is past. Now comes the lent of my long hate. For. The elephant only allows himself to be led by drivers whom he has adopted. And. It's the French who say, When the Devil gets old, he becomes pious.

The monster who bares her breast from the balcony on Bourbon. And. The man in the mask and the skeleton costume. But. If the time between. The Box. The Ash. The Rabbit. And the Hat. Your whirling dervish slows on still numbers. Our Mother screams from the apex of old Ferris. And. Our Clown is brought to tears again. As. You stand in vertical anticipation. And I, seeking the accident of your attention, climb horizontal into the box and wait for the onslaught of carnage.

Hollow cloth over a hand. Or. Five fingers in a head of wood. As. A figure moved by human fingers. And. Stiffer effigies have no moving parts. As. My mouth is mere decoration. Or. My mandible operable by manipulation. Like my eyelids that open and close. These are my hinges. Those are your hands. And. More flexible fabrics are stuffed. Like. The thumb that enters the inner pocket. For. A body no longer than the length between your hand and your elbow. It's your arm that my body hangs over.

From manus, hand. As. Moses held up his. Or. You hold up yours as you stand in a narrow booth. The instrument of the brain. As distinguished from the brute. The terminal parts beyond the wrists. Or. The power of husbands over wives. I am suffering by the hands of the hangman. At a loss to discover what hand the moon has. While. Your floor is covered in Suns. I have been dealt a bad one. As. A pointer which indicates the divisions of a clock. Or. A body bag.

And. Puppet. From. The later form of poppet. As. Dummy. Doll. An idol. An insect between larva and adulthood. For. This is the Punch and Judy show. And. You are beating me to death again. Or. You speak through a squeaker and give me a shrill inhuman timbre. I can only be justified by adding the unnatural. You've forgotten my eyes. Or. Forgotten to dot my eyes and nose.

This is the country of puppets. And. Peacocks are sold in boxes. The Devil may buy my soul for a puppet show. The one where Goethe first saw Faust. I want a poppet of you to put my pins in. But. You float me down the holy river with a prayer. The length of time I stay afloat shows you how kindly. See. The gods are all judging me now.

An expression whose meaning is not compositional. A grammatical construction whose connotation does not follow the denotation. A figure of speech. A colloquial metaphor. Deeply rooted and traceable. For. Word forms peculiar to a people. Own tongue. Or. I wish you to frame all sentences in their mother phrase. And. To allow every polysyllable word one long time. The Latin style and antique picture frames. Which fall into tongues most aptly. For. District dialect. Particular parlance. Linguistic patois. And. Departure from the strict syntactical rules. But. If to bring something to light is in an Idiom of the English Tongue, you are putting a rabbit to me. While I am trying to put words into your shell. But. I am dreaming in saws. For. The language of Neutrality is entirely based on the principle of internationality. And. The linguistic club of Nuremberg is remarkable for having gone through the evolution from Volapük to Idiom Neutral. Via Esperanto.

So we may say, This is Christ's body, by the communication of Idiom to bread. Or. Idiotism. The common speak. Some patchery bungled up in uplandish Idiom. Or. Adverbial use of the Attribute and Apposite. And. The Tennessee twang. Both Spanglish and Technospeak. The genius of jargon. For. The word *idioma* means language. Here is the form of a horn. And. The Histories of all our former Wars are transmitted to us in the Vernacular. As. Divine sparks that glow.

Specific property. Distinctive nature. Peculiarity. As. Impartial Judge, save present state, Truth's Idiom of things past. For. Who can look upon those wondrous idioms reserved for your eyes? A technical term of science or art. As. Tate has much to offer when he finds his way out of the Eliot idiom. And. Ellington's music had its origins in New Orleans, as has much in the jazz idiom. But. If to bring something to light is in an Idiom of the English Tongue, I ask you to stop pulling wool. Keep me as the apple of your eye. Hide me in the shadow of your wing. For. I am secretary to the commissions of idiocy. Having stars. And. By this Rule, Clemency and Tyranny should signify the same Thing.

A vertically reciprocating saw driven by a rapid crank. One which cuts in contours and curves. Or. A type of architectural decoration. A set of funny pieces which, when assembled, form an image or a map. The puzzle so named because the picture, attached to wood or paperboard, is cut into complication. Originally, an educational device for the teaching of geography. As. A dissected map of England. The band has driven it mostly out of use. And. The hand. Adapted for sawing scrolls and frets. These are the jigsaw days. And. Bargework is often made with the jig. The gingerbread and the steamboat Gothic. For. The late Victorian era saw the saw in aggravation. And. Salad forks are cut without markings. But. If the principal use of the saw is to divide wood, you jigsaw longitudinally, through my thickness. You are showing your serrated teeth. While. I am trying to jigsaw the pieces of our past. The puzzle of the present. For. It's the saw that moves backwards and forwards through time.

From jig. To gambol, to freak, to sport. To leap, to kick, wanton. Hear the onomatopoetic influence. For. A rude fiddle. A lively dance. As. I suppose you and I are to stand up and jig again. Much like wounded fish. And. The beau monde is bobbing. Don't think the gloss of your smooth evasion shall jig me off. For. To shape an earthen vessel. To bore with a spring pole. The ore is given to the child. Who shakes it in a sieve. But. Until the sad Catastrophe shows, this is but mockery and mirth. For. The jig is up. The die is cast. The fat is decidedly in the fire. And. Every soul aboard has hung a piece of painted lead. Like the jiggy ribs of half-opened umbrellas.

And. Saw. Ordinarily, the complete instrument. With defining words, indicating special forms. As. The band saw, compass saw, drag saw, endless. Fret saw, gate saw, keyhole. And. Faction, hatred, liver, emulation. Here are the serrated anima. The saws of the soul. As. There you see the saw of mountain peaks against the black and blue sky.

Scarcely is there so peppery a person with such constant inclination. Didn't I tell you? The bears are eating berries. The palmetto lies under the pine. As. We've crawled out into the open and hissed. For. The sound of our love-notes bears a great resemblance to the noise. But. Because the ghost cannot hand the saw, it is of little to no avail. For. It's the sawfish that torments the Whale.

A building for habitation and habit. Or. Headquarters of a domicile. A dwelling place of a family. Or. A structure that serves as shelter. As. A burrow or nest or cave. A shack in a series of shacks. With nooks and garrets and stairs. This is your corner of the world. Thick with suspicious walls. Or. I am backpedaling through my Motionless Childhood. For. A box for the keeping of birds. A place of worship. As. A church. Entertainment. As. A tavern. For. To be quit of you I confine myself to the house. Or. I am living alone in such emptiness. Burying my Lares in the basement. But. If this house should come to ruin, I am trying hard to fix the dispersed days. When you haunted this house of horror. Or. I am furnishing my house with memory. As. Locomotives and other forgettings.

Inmates collectively. For. A daughter who brings the house down. The harder shell of a snail. Or. A tortoise. As. The swallow builds its own indent. Of wood, or stone, or clay. Protection from weather. Protection again from time. The first principle of architecture. From which all things extend. But. Until you hit the boy in the back with a bottle, this is but a barroom box. Where six tall men play gilded guitars. Two which ways and ever which time. For. These are my lullaby lies. And. This house has memory of home.

The I and the not I. As. Protection of I. Divisions of the brain. For. A receptacle of any kind. A twelve parts of heaven. Or. The entire sky. Excepting parts that never rise. For. A sign of the zodiac is considered the seat. Where artificers may be heard. But. If seven children play at house, fireside things lie in the brush. Or. What is more beautiful than a road? A roof and a roost. A den and my digs. I am confined as by illness. To stay in this house without purpose.

A deltoid diamond in the sky. Or. An isosceles triangle. A frame of wood with stretched fabric and a tail. Or. A toy flown in high winds by means of a string. For the purpose of raising weights. Hoisting flags. And. A bird of prey having a forked tail and no tooth. As. Buzzard or bald kite. Long-winged flying Hawk. And. The carcass that lies to be devoured by kite and by crow. Or. A person who rapaciously preys. A sharper. More indefinitely. A term of detestation. And. A letter smuggled into or out of prison. For. The highest sails of a ship set only in light wind. Spinnaker. But. If the kite must conform to the laws of aerodynamics, you notice the similarity between powered sparks and lightning. Between thunder and the crackling sound of. Electricity. You send your wired kite into the splendid sky and tie a skeleton to the string. You. Raise it in the gathering thunderstorms. While I. Make a diamond of my love letters, all seven hundred odd. String them together in the weaker winds. For. Letters of my confession. My letters of concession. And *Culpa* is imputable to defect of the intellect. *Dolus* to defects of the heart.

A dud check drawn from a dud book. For. It's the bird kite that frightens partridges. And. A name for a variety of Almond Tumbler Pigeons having. Black plumes and red webs of feathers. As. The Almond and the Kite will produce exactly one Almond and one Kite. No related word appears in the cognate languages. But. If the kite must conform to the laws of aerodynamics, you are responsible for grounding the angrier gods. I turn on my radio. Drive divisively into the wind. For. I am trying to discover which way this world is blowing.

A Babylon of knots and blind alleys. Or. A design to confine a Bullman. A simple spiral. A little petroglyph. Convoluted courts and chambers. And. A maze. With reference to the structures so named. Or. A temple at the entrance of the lake. A double axe. Connoting place. For. Although the complex palace has not been found, something is being shown to visitors. As. Entanglement. Morass. Inextricable condition. For. If our house by writers was so called, you have given me the gift of honey. Named me Lady of the Labyrinth. And. Ensnared me in this flower with your monster. But. If labyrinth is to gardening as rebus is to poetry, I am trying to embrangle your soul in mine. Or. I am lost in the lachrymose language. While. The purple clefts of your affection are labyrinthed in such darkness.

If labyrinth is to gardening as rebus is to poetry, a leafy maze of high hedges and complex canals. Anatomically, the knotted veins and arteries traveling to and from the heart. Or. The cavity of the inner ear. Resembling the Shell of a Snail. Metallurgically, a chamber of turnings for the condensation of fumes. And. Ornithologically, the membranous capsule which encloses. Here. The auditory nerves of birds. For.

A jungle, a knot, a mesh. A web, a puzzle, a riddle. Or. A mare's nest. And. A rat's. Wheels within wheels. Traps for malevolent spirits. Paths for ritual dances. The more difficult path to God and the Devil. See. The roofs are made wholly of stone. While. The basements house crocodile tombs. I thought I was at the finish. But my way was bent. And. Now I am back at the beginning. Or. You have lost all sense of hearing. Ensnared me in fullness with your infection. But. I have seen your tortuous heart. With six different centers and a great many stops. And. Like the geometer without practice, I fall into manifold errors. For. Perciform fish of the suborder Anabantoidei. As. Siamese fighting fish, the Kissing Gourami, and Paradise.

Mirror

A ditto. A double. A dupe. A characteristic deserving imitation. Or. A distinction deserving avoidance. For. A looking glass of both saints and sinners, born from the same conundrum. As. Language is the mirror of society. Media, the mirror of the mind. And. Follow the example of Christian Kings. Free from Clouds of Flattery. For. A reflective surface. A polished metal. Slippery silver and lyric aluminum. For. Such as the stuff of mirror backs. Mercury is also employed. Hear the mingling of fish. As. A piece of cloth having sheen. An oval ornament having borders. And. If. Or. But. If dreams are meant to mirror the night, I am standing in the hall. Your face is nailed to the wall. I am watching. Your lens is burning. For. A pyrobolic Mirror Glass also casts fire. And. Improvements in machinery multiply. Your darkish, bricky, London-like streets.

A circular region in the wings of crickets. As. A resonator for higher frequencies. In angling, short for mirror carp. As. The mirror-backed globes are preferable to those painted. Or. A wall bracket supporting branches, backed for the enhancement. But. If dreams are meant to mirror the day, I am wearing a gown of grey. While you are knotting your unblack tie. See. By you, everything is done with smoke. Not by magic or by miracle. But by the patch of white on the wings of gulls.

A fugue that is played in inversion. The eyes of fish in death. Seven hundred cattle with awaiting the execution. As. Oars keep time on waters. And. Blue patterned chairs flank the mantel. I am the self-betrayed mirrorgazer. For. According to Lacan, the earliest game is that of identification. With the body. Or. I am the self-betrayed mirrorgazer. For. You are my looking glass lake and I am bending my body. The stars alight in your stillness. Or. You are making me clown again. I am the talk of the town again. As. The willow sees the heron upside down.

Vertical light bundled on the horizon. Or. Horizontal light swept. As. An aid for navigation and pilotage. Or. A tower with powerful lamps and erected at a dangerous point. Near the unsafe sea for the guidance of mariners. In former times, a fire. Kindled on a hill. A beacon. Or. A seabed structure. Used to indicate tortuous coasts and hazardous shoals. From light. That which is bright. The natural agent of the luminary sun. And. House. Building of habit and habitation. But. If beyond a certain intensity, light ceases to be luminous and becomes a mere partner of pain, you shine too brightly in my eyes. You are my whitehouse. My beacon. My pharos. Or. Perhaps I am darkening. As the lighthouse will that turns upon the sea. So. Listen now. Tow the lighthouse out to sea and sink it in the seabed. Then. Fill the base with hourglass sand. For. The lighthouse man is missing. Or. This is a modern unmanned house.

As. Opposed to darkness. The deeper delusion. As. Darkness from light we part on two. Concentration is accomplished by rotating lenses. In older lighthouses, the lamp and lenses were rotated by clockwork assembly. Floated in mercury to reduce friction. Now. Omnidirectional flashes are similar to those aerobeacons that warn fliers from skyscrapers. For. Candlepower is expressed in candelas. Intensities vary from thousands to millions. But. If the range depends upon atmosphere and elevation, your light looms on the line. Is scattered by particles of water. This is your nominal range.

But. I've seen your light and you don't steadily burn. You rhythmic eclipsing provides code. Identification. This is your character. The interval of repetition, your period. For. You are painted white against the open sea. With conspicuous bands of black. You are too visible, invisible, and that is why you play this part. For. You have shown yourself and I can no longer see. The blinded lookout on this bucket, I am drowning in the seaside sea. While. The memory of you emerges from the night. Like. Cornflowers that rain over my heart.

An invented code. Or. A system of signaling. A set of symbols representing letters. As. An alphabet of long and short. Written as dash and dot. And. Patterns of punctuation. The patent is null and void. And. I am tapping out gibberish. Pressing and releasing. Operating buttons. Elaborating ways to make my communication clear. By which my message can be flashed to ships. As. A series of flashing lights. Lacking code. The radiotelegraph and the amateur radio. Or. A spark. For. S.O.S. is so easily transmitted. As. Save Our Souls. Triplets of dot and dash. And. Dot again. But. If the signifier for distress is due to the ease of its transmission, a dash is three times as long as a dot. And. This is my internal space. My inter character space is longer. As. The dash. And. The spaces between the words are. Dot dot dot to seven.

So. Axes swing and hammers sing. Ellipses and et ceteras. Fireflies flash their blink-a-blink blink. Or. Night bugs clack their click click click. And. The river. As it signals. In morse. About omega. But. If the signifier of distress is due to the ease of the signal, I am operating buttons. As. From a bonny rose. Ditto with regard. Or. I am embossing the instrument with a movable magnet. For. This is my construction.

A walrus of the same seal. A hippopotamus behemoth. Or. Waves written by siphons above central. There I go again. Morseing my name again. Or. Morseing my distress. Landing in Darwin. Or. I am reading your message loud and clear. Dear S.O.S. Dear et cetera. In your full silence with fuller stops. I am reading your message loud and clear. From the ratta-tap-tap of the blind man.

A piece of waste. Or. An unowned land. A desolate area. Or. A place on a boundary. Beyond the boundary. Between two boundaries. As. The ground outside of London used for executions. Or. A space amidships. Midway between the bow and the stern. The forecastle and the booms. Beyond the sunset. Beyond the baths. Or. Midway between the afterpart of the belfry and the forepart of. Between the trenches. Blanketed with bombs. And. Riddled with landmines and wire. This is a sea of explosions. For the storage of ropes and blocks. But. If you buy the ground between us and enclose it in this Brick, I am dying of a high fever. Or. I am walking on a wager from No Man's Land to the World's End. For. This is my life. This is my town. I am the nomad and this my no-go area. But. You have armed yourself with tanks. Your Trojan Horses. For. Until the World War, Hell remained largely impenetrable.

Terra nullius. The world where no one lives. Or. Plot not under sovereign control. Politically organized. As. Saguia el-Hamra. Rio de Oro. Laredo. And. Liancourt Rocks. But. If you buy the ground between us, I have said that I am dying. Or. I am boxing empty air. For. I'm training for a fight long planned. With Nobody. For love at No Man's Land.

Drive a ball far into the backhand corner of these badlands. Or. A bomb. For. Time and again, you drive the world. As. I am headed somewhere over the rainbow. Brandishing my nom de guerre. For. The marshland eligible for building upon. Wetlands, badlands, boondocks, and backwoods. A half a rood of rock. This is my no-fly zone. Or. An imaginary place. A state of confusion. Time and again, I return like a cobra to crawl. For. Midway on our life's journey, I found myself in the dark woods. The right road lost.

A semisolid substance used as a salve. An emollient. A medicament. Or. A medicinal preparation in the form of paste. A concoction used for ceremonial anointment. As. Viscous oil from the ghost. An unction. An unguent. A cream or a balm. A toiletry made of substances having a moisturizing effect. But. If the irritation is severe, you are the patron saint of pharmacy. With your spatula. Your urine flask. And. I am the patron saint of firefighting. With a stone around my neck in the river. Underwater. For. A flint glass and a nickel cap. You have the ointment box. Or. You are the ointment maker. Mixing fragments of sun until it becomes unguent. Then. Adding rhodium.

See. Poetry is not a paganism. Sweet anointment of the holy. Physicians are rolling pills. And. Making mud of. This is my body blank. Or. Life-drops. Is dropping. Of a sovereign virtue to repel the heat.

As. Camphor. A gummy solid. Flammable and volatile. Of a formula. For use in ammunition and plastics. Insecticides and medicine. And. Derived from a Taiwanese tree. I ask you, How? You say, See here. Cook its wood and condense its vapor. Then. Cook its crystals with quicklime. Condensing again into gum. Or. Refine turpentine to make pinene. Pass it quickly through a prickly pipe. Then blend it all with hydrogen chloride. At settings and at pressures. For the making of flakes.

But. There's a fly in my ointment. Or. A trifling circumstance which spoils enjoyment. A thing that detracts from agreeableness. For. Canopus was a centre of the industry and a pleasure resort for Alexandrians. Osiris was worshiped at Canopus as a human headed vessel. And. The Canopic jar is used to hold the entrails of a mummy. But. I am off topic. Or. I am sidestepping the ointment. For. I've sent away my Mercury with a fly in his ear. A fly thus enclosed in amber.

A machine for weaving. And. Bars and beams fixed in place. To form a frame. Or. Hold parallel threads in alternating sets. As. Raise the warp to run the weft. Where the wenches weave their shadows. Beneath the shade of blooming trees. Of linen, wool, or ribbon. Both the hand and the power. The circle and the draw. Or. Any tool of any kind. For. Thread is woven into fabric. Look. Here smokes your Castle. There it fumes. While. Here upon your Ship. The Ocean looms.

If the loom is not level, turn it 90 degrees and check again. For. All your looms of Ionia are kept in such grace to supply your glowing body with long purple robes. And. A spider or a caterpillar. Poetic for the web. And. My hands are all tombs. Of sticking-wicks and weir-like looms. While. Your men are thrown over. Over as they stand. And. My fatal sisters glitter glances. Weaving all the sailors' doom.

An open vessel of any kind. Bucket, tub, and vat. A vessel or a boat. And. The beam of an oar. Between the blade and the handle. Moon beam. Loom beam. Pertaining to the fathoms. Mast as big which yet. Where your mother too sends her loom-bred men. Magnified to mountains. From the ship. To the line.

See. I am trying to leave this room. Where. Woven waters seem to fall. As trees, and beasts, and will. This is my flesh. Or. That is a diver. Black at the crown. Snow-white at the belly. On the water near the rocks. In the company of razors. For. In the slowness of the silence. I am weaving the cloth of your country. I have said I'm trying to leave this room. Like a ship from the fog. A seaman's term for the indistinct appearance. As. No mirage of tradition give characters their loom. And. Slowly up. Slowly down. As. A ship under sail. Looming like a lion. When the wind is sure to blow.

Birdcage of the Muses. Or. Boundlessness of universe. School dedicated. Building set. House ordained. For. This is the delicate study of philosophy. Art and its letters. And. The tragedy of conversation. Of epics and of poetry. Or. Motley menagerie of the outmoded. Repository for the useless. Held and exhibited. And. Odor of abominations. Of myrrh and of frankincense. For. The body of Man is a museum of the obsolete. My anatomy. And. I wander ghostlike through this Museum of Mirrors. This world is a mirage. While you wander through the porticos of Alexandria. Headed by the president-priest. For. The pretty little larva clad in stiff hair that eats the bodies of your bugs is called the Museum Beetle. I leave only the severed wings of your infamous insects. The pins and their labels. For. I doubt there is anything of value. As. Everything is worthless. In the Wax Museum of Your Waning Illumination.

The Louvre and The Guggenheim. The Whitney and The Tate. The Tech Museum of Innovation. And. The Holocaust. As. Memorial to the murdered. For. These are the dioramas of the unmarried daughters of Memory. And. Differentiation is a matter of mythological systematization rather than of the cult. For. Statues were a popular decoration in the galleries. And. Sculptors gave to each daughter a fanciful attribute.

Muse of poetry. Muse of history. Muse of lyric and of love. I am dancing to a melancholy music. Inspired by the resinous replicas of serial killers. Three tiny scenes of the Plague. Bone skulls covered in wax. And. Venus who can be dismantled. This is a tragedy. But. You find me funny. For. A storehouse for old treasures. Mausoleum for the monuments. The salaries of the staff are paid by the Egyptian kings. And. Promontory for ruins and souvenirs. For. *Je me souviens. Mais. Tu m'as oubliée. Et. Je voudrais m'endormir et ne jamais me réveiller.*

A person. A place. A thing. A class or category. Or. A unique entity. In early use, with qualifying adjective. As. Noun essential. Noun substantive. Sir being the masculine. Her poetry is round. Rife with rhyme and noun substantives. Both the subject and the object. From *nomen*. A Roman. Both the man and the mouse. The elephant and the house. Or. An omen. This is the language of habit and habitation. And. The hangover only reached us from America. See. One is a noun. Two is a noun. We are a noun. And. Instantiation shadows the copulative *is*. But. If there is a prototypical association between the noun and the first-order entity, I am placing the verb out of order. Too far back behind the noun. Or. Death is a clown. As yet declined. And. We find the War of Worlds to be a War of Words.

The system of classes is characteristic to the Congo. Marked by an affix. Signaling a singular. Or. The plural. As. I saw the plural rise. Or. Both the prefix and the suffix. And. The accompanying concord. So. In the sentence, *wa-tu wa-le wa-mefika*, consisting of a noun, demonstrative, and verb, concords link the entities. The *tu* and the *le*.

Adjective Clauses are born by the Relative Pronoun. Referring to the Antecedent. Implied in the Principal. Certain suffixes denote inferiority and worthlessness. And. Those of the superlative degree require a Genitive. So. Frighten the child is a verb. But. If there is an association between the noun and the entity, you are only abstract. Or. I am Nounless. A noun-like township. The state or quality of being something. As. We suffer the nounless verb-tongue of the Impossible Marriage. This is our circumlocution. That is our redundancy. A tautology. Or. How many nouns of asking haste? But. If we suffer the language of Us, substances like water are difficult to count. And. Compounds with wolf are used by warriors.

The art of dancing. Or. A semicircular section in front of a proscenium. Elegant and commodious. And. Reserved for the seats of senators. As. The Noblest Seats of Heaven. Or. The section between the stage and the common area. Between the chorus and the instrumentalists. Space set apart for the musicians. Thumbed by the brilliantined leader. For. This is a trombone. That is the Man That Got Away. I dance at the cemetery center. Land at the foot of my hero. For. The balalaika bellows from below. Or. The Yeats is more economical. Reduced in fat to three players. Seven soloists and a semisubstantial mix. But. If the orchestra harbors every bowed vibration, this is your Sentimental Journey. And. These are my soft explosions. For. I am sitting alone again, fat fists clapping. As heaven chants amen to man.

Impatient sticks in pits. And. Catcalls in the gallery. Or. A flexible construction with a high-tech cockpit. Or. Music mingles with the hum of your voice. Those quarter-tone wavers and ostinato poundings. Like a folding of wheat. And. A rustling of rubles. While I am gurgling from my winter cave. Cutting your sentences into songs. For. This is the declaration of that paradox that self-homicide is not naturally a sin. And. That it shall never be otherwise.

While. A battery of big drums drum. And. The piccolo's impish shrill. Ovals echo while the oboe's plaintiff pastoral. See. This is a different pitch. That is a clarinet. No. You are taking your place in the semicircle of stars. For. The sky is your canopy. But. It's raining again. Half a tone higher and a quarter beat faster. Or. The piano is plucking and I am paying the price. As. Thunder rumbles. The child giggles. And. Birds come in from the trees.

Loss of life liberties. And. The locale in which locking is ensured. A system of separation. A system of silence. And. The world arranged for the lawless and the wrong. As. He may not break from prison until the Devil's dead. And. The defendant was persistent in saving his wife from life. The word appears to have arisen from a person taken into captivity in times of war. Thus considered a successful capture. A possession. Or. A prize. Prismatic. But. If the punishment is supposed to fit the crime, I sit isolated in the cellblock of your affection. Listening to the clang and bang of your inattention. For. I am trying hard to practice good behavior. To parole myself from your all-seeing eye. While you. Succeed in all-regulating rule. You are my world and my warden. For. In Roulette, the position on the board where bets are held in abeyance. As. When the spinner lands on Zero, even stakes aren't scooped. They are impounded. I am imprisoned. For. This land is your land. And. Alcatraz is not an island.

Beantown. Can. Clink. And cooler. Cell and slammer. Joint and jug. Both lockup and lockdown. For. A prisoner can be both jailer and the person jailed. And. The child is now tried as an adult. But. If the punishment is supposed to fit the crime, you allow me no chance of escape. For. Behind the fast bars of your incarcerating heart, I confess that I am guilty. Spare me the guillotine. Of trying to make a paradise of your prison.

With hyphenation, of or pertaining to jails. As. Prison-cell. Prison-clock. Prison-dream. Or. Instrumental locative. As. Prison-born. Prison-bound. Prison-made. A prison-bird is a person who is often and at length imprisoned for felonies. For. You venture to ask me who I am. And. I venture to reply. Nothing but a prison-bird. I watch the prison-clock smite upon the shivering air. For. With sentence. Time served.

The action of asking. Or. The stating of a problem. An inquiry. Into. A matter. Discourse of doubt. Expression of the uncertain. Or. Conversation on qualms. For. If to be is what be questing. Fortune crowns. To be beyond is to be without. And. A wavering. Fixing full on my face. As. The application of torture. And. Attempts to process answers. As. This time, it's the American who must come forward. For. The question is the subject of strife. But. If the error of a monk is responsible for the switching of *h* and *w*, a compound. Composite. Thus. Because in Spanish, sounds harden, you ask me. *¿Quien eres tu? ¿Que hac hecho con mi corazon?* But. You are calling for ambiguity. While I am calling for an alleviation of this confusion. A disambiguation. So. I ask you. Am I suffering now?

To interrogate. With double. I am like nighttime. Questing stars for myself. Or. A murmuring. A putting of questions to God. See. Socrates was condemned to death by hemlock. Now. You are interrupting me. Or. You are raising objections. From quest. A crowner. As. The quest comes in and says, Guilty. And. I am forbidden the feat. But. If the error of monks changes the sound of your voice, a set of persons employed in searching. As. Twelve brave mermen for a quest.

The catechism. As. The search for game by hounds. Or. The giving of tongue in pursuit of birds. There's a wild bee questing honey buds. Or. A bark. As. You are my answer. I am your unsolved problem. And. To press and to squeeze. Hearts are said to be quested. Those whose sides have been crushed. I cannot answer myself, to render anything dark. A mark of interrogation. Represented by a sign. And. A stand up curl with a straighter stem. Like a quaver in music. But. It is your question that disturbs my dreams. Then. Ask me no questions and I'll tell you no lies. Until when we have kissed at quests and commands.

Writing of the illuminations. Or. An image made by mechanical eyes. A likeness or delineation. Or. The application of Light to the purpose of Representation. Rather. The smallest reduction of the largest pyramid. And. The largest enlargement of the smallest microbe. An underwater waterlog of the sawfish in swim. For. If the rays of light reflected from these earthly bodies cause a chemical reaction, you choose to travel the world in hot air balloons and record the shapes of the greater plains. You. Strap the camera to your wing and make maps of the unborn clouds. You point with precision your submerged lens and make a photo of the fathoms. While I. Entrapped in dim redness of this dark room, struggle to fix your frame on the second dimension plane. For. I am trying hard to make eternal your ephemeral face. I beg you to consider a stiller life. For. As the shutter opens and closes, I find that the only difference between the atom and the atom bomb. Is exposure time.

The action depends on the same principles as the fading of rugs in the sun. Now there are wonderfully sensitive chemicals that change their nature with speed. As. Silver salts and bromide. But. If the rays of light reflected from these earthly bodies cause a chemical reaction. I ask you to look natural. Make me the focus of your panorama. For. I am trying to show you the memory of my mirage. And. In a minute or so you will see the black patches of negative space. Then. The outline of your jaw.

The brush, the palette, the colors, the craft, the practice, the patience, the glance, the touch, the paste, the glaze, the trick, the relief, the finishing, the rendering. Murderer of the classical arts. And.

Never ready for. Use the technology that. Get the cameraman for all I see is this fog. And. Never ever have I slept with the door so tightly closed. Or. Paper smeared with solution of a lunar caustic. And. The stationary bullet fixed whizzing through the air. And. A mushroom cloud blown big. Actively, to produce the negative fixed in Forever. For. Because a single flash is worth more than one thousand, I would like to collect you in my album. This book without language. I am trying hard to make you the Always of my Never Mind. From light blue to midnight. Or sepia.

A character representing sound. Or. A machine invented by Thomas Edison by which noise is recorded and reproduced. And. An instrument capable of being attached to pianofortes and organs by means of which they are rendered. Melographic. Capable of writing any music played upon them. For. If the instrument makes probable this oral hallucination, you spin the record of your reddened choice. Or. You mimic the melody and its blank harmony. You accompany the symphony with a tenor of all tomorrows. While I, lost in the Maze of Mirrors, ask you to tell me again the story.

You say, First. You say, Make. First, make your mouth make a sound. Speak into the mouthpiece and cause the tremors in the thin diaphragm. Then. The steel point makes tracings upon the hard wax. Fix the thing upon a spinning cylinder. And. By means of the tracings, the diaphragm will repeat with perfection your original voice. Or. The echoes in the mountains of your lamentations. As. Cries in a haunted brothel. Or. Whispers in a ghostly tavern. The instrument has spoken in our hearing. Listen. It is a natural outcome of the telephone. Listen. The old man's laugh comes to us as out of a phonograph.

I say, Perfect. I say, Yet. This instrument warbles. And. This record is warped. And. The tongue of this snake. Has scratched this disk. For. Your voice is skipping. And. As I put the conch to my same hear, I listen to the echo of. I listen to the echo of. The raspy susurrations of your *adieu*.

Applied to a person or thing that exactly reproduces the utterances of another person or thing. Hence, the transitive verb. To report in Pitman's phonograph. As. It is a great loss to me that your song was not phonographed and preserved. And. Whether it be so, it is phonographed in the mind of the mindful God. All out of sync.

Telegraphy without wire. German Telefunken. Or. Distant sparks. And. Transmission and reception of radiofrequency electromagnetic flutterings. Frequencies are stated in cycles of hertz. As. A frequency of seven kilohertz is 7000 flutters per second. A megahertz is one million. Or. Organized wireless broadcasting. As a medium of communication. Sending messages to ships at sea was one of its first uses. Now. Signals about conditions that influence the weather are received from high flying balloons. Or. As art. This is Radio Chaos. And. In the middle of the country, I have heard both the Atlantic and Pacific surfs. On the radio. But. If science has made it made it possible for me to blazon my disembodied broadcast, I drop my bottle into stiller waters. Watch it bob toward your infected ear. For. Signals are created by the oscillating electric currents. And. You need to be both strengthened and converted.

The action of these waves compare to the action of waves on water. But. Radio waves are not shaped like water waves. And. It's the radio that goes to war. As. Berlin radio relies on divisive propaganda. Moscow radio announces that Russia has launched an earth satellite. Cairo radio interprets the Soviet warning to Britain as a threat to bomb London. And. Soldiers carry his tiny talkies on their helmets. While. Miniature transmitter are swallowed to broadcast signals according to the body. In the evening, we listen to the radio and play billiards. See the set of expanding domes.

This is a test. This is only a test. And. Radio antenna. Apparatus. Beacon. And. Intercept again. For. While I fly contentedly checking my direction by the radio beacons, I ask Goose Bay if they have any other traffic. Pronunciation is not an opportunity for elegance but a problem of what to do with words. If this were an actual emergency, I think I said "I love you." As I cut off the radio link.

Umbrella

A piece of fabric stretched on ribs that radiate from a central spine. Or. A portable screen used for protection. A circumference supported on a stick. Against rain. Against sun. Or. A canopy of silk, carefully hooped and extended. This is a parasol. Monstrously yellow. Part and parcel of. In Palermo. See. These are the Baubles of China. Extended in a rounded compass. Or. That is a Hair Ring. Your own stately Picture. As. A symbol of rank. A symbol of Dignity. And. Upon your Throne are placed two grand umbrellas, the handles of which are nine feet high. But. If it requires a good umbrella to protect men from death, I am arching my back again. Spreading myself open like an umbrella. Like. The radiating rays of the sun. But. The sky is pouring rain again. And. This engine is broken again. And. I am your brainsick fool. Unsheltered from your grand scorches of censure. Maladapted by your discontent. For. The grand umbrella your dark foliage casts an impenetrable shade.

A dome and a cloak. A tent and a tarp. When this rain recedes, find me in the Garden with Sloping Walls. For. A sunblind. As. To keep off stuff from the Window. A curtain of fast American fighters. Above the harbor. And. Serving for protection. Against rain. Against sun. But. If it requires a good umbrella to protect men from death, you are swinging your closed enclosure like a walking stick. Singing in pouring the rain. While. Doves, like umbrellas, all their feathers nightly shed.

A broad-brimmed hat. Or. A parachute. The cap of the gemstone mushroom. The gelatinous disk of a jelly. And. The elder tree. As. The epitome of eternal order. A fan. Or. A flytrap. And. The government under which criminal sins are committed. For. The bird is about the size of a crow. Decorated with a crest of curlicue feathers. Which, when raised, spread themselves like. I am arching my back again. A shade before your bolded body. Or. A shell, Limpet-like, and marked by concentric lines. And. A furled fan.

A game of chance. Or. A gambling sport. As. Wheel of Fortune. Wheel of Fame. Or. A glamorous attraction in Monte Carlo. Differently colored. Indicating the players. Not the values. Not exactly. Or. A game played on a revolving concave table. Onto which a ball. Into which a box. Or. The rolling of balls is central. For. A banking game at the Birdcage Alehouse. At the Rising Sun. Where the bets are placed against the bank. Upon the red. Or. Upon the black. As. Invented by monks. Or. Invented by the Chinese and communicated by monks. For. The ball has no memory. The name of the game is blame. To you, I am a bit of fun. A frolic. A joke. A lark. To me, you are the croupier. Of Russian Roulette. But. If the ball has no memory, it falls into the same slot seven times running. Or. You whirl the wheel counterclock. These are the anti-turnings of time. Then. Toss the ball from three to six. For. This is a whirlpool. Or. This is a whirlwind. All bets are against me. And. The most common system is the Martingale. Where. All bets are doubled. I am taking to losing again. And. You have the advantage. For. Wherever there is likely to be Friction, you are playing the game with me.

Straight. Split. Street. Or. Square. Line as six. Column as dozen. It's like I said before. This is a tornado. Dozens low. Or. Dozens high. Noir or Rouge. Diamonds are taking the place of words again. Odds or even. Paired. Impaired.

A device to keep the hair in curl. So. Put the wig in pipes. Pile it in a pyramid of rolls. Add some pads, some puffs, and some pins. Or. An expeditious way of multiplying dots. One like a spur rowel. Another at right angles. Used to raise the burr when the cradle has been burned. Or. A toothed wheel for perforating postage stamps. So. If this be Play, let's begin the Diversion. The wheel is spinning the room again. Roly-poly. Or. A Country Dance. For. You have dollar signs for eyes again. And. Chances are. House odds.

A rod, a cord, a wire. Or. The life of the taller clocks. With a weight at one. By position, in relation. Or. A body suspended from fixation. So it swings under the influence. On an arc. To the Earth. The period is the pulse. By position, in relation. Or. Never. But. If the strength of gravity is not entirely uniform, I am swaying faster and shorter. Or. You thought it not amiss to sway me longer and slower. For. I am suspended from the pin of your indecision. This is the pivot of your full stop. Or. The interval of time itself. For. A rock tied to a rope. A plumb at the end of a string. Or. The swing itself. As. Hours. Minutes. Seconds. But. If the strength of gravity is not entirely uniform, your gait is as regular as a pendulum. Or. I am all bump and bone. For. My pendulous feet don't reach the ground. As. The shaky trapeze artist wavers.

One of the best measures of gravity. So. Fire a cannon into the clock to measure the speed of the shot. A rod resting in a socket. For. This is the end of music. As connected, by relation. As. Bulrushes knock at my knees. I am left nothing but rocking. In the unanchored, marshy bottom.

If anyone has an occasion for time, let them repair to the sign. This is the wisdom of ministers. Or. That is a vibration. I am drumming between laughter and tears. Conveying the century in hammocks. For. I am regulated by an engine. As. The saw that cuts as it swings.

The escape wheel of a clock. Or. The balance wheel of a watch. The wire's composed of flats. As. Interpose the chain and the cam in the manner. So. Raise your eyes to the old brass. Without the time or peace of mind. For. The sound of your heart is like beats. Evenly spaced and placed. For. I have a theory. The stones are all falling loose again. The bough is breaking the cradle. And. This time, it is I who suffer the punishment in the gully.

I have a theory. For. I have heard the unmistakable twang. Now the bob is missing. The spring is broken. The shaky trapeze artist falls. And. I don't think this rule applies to happiness. I am suffering the punishment in the gully. Or. The adversary name of Troy.

A nautical triangular sail. Or. A high-standing bonnet. An unusually tall man. Or. A horse. Sired by Highflier and who won the Epsom Derby. And. That Skyscraper mare who made Brainworm by Buzzard. An exaggeration. And. A tall tale. As. My yellowed yarn can't come well after your skyscraper of love. Or. A high-rider of high-cycles typical of antiquity. Architecturally, a building of many stories. Especially those characteristic to. Cosmopolitan conurbations. And. The most American thing in the world. For. If the developments of steel and concrete make possible the construction of eternally tall buildings, you reside in the penthouse of paradise. Power is a cabaret cult. And. Your nowadays name is Profit. But. I am impeded by your skyscraper eyes. Or. I bide my time in the longer lingers of your penumbra. For. My world is turning. And. I beg you to tell me. Who are these men who eternally build?

A composite of sky. As. Cloud. Arch of the counterfeit heavens. Or. The firmament. As. The sky is a careless place to dwell. And. The sky is the natural habitat of the unnatural airplane. Put that in your rocket pocket. With. Scraper. As. Unscrupulous plunderer. Cathouse fiddler. Blue-blooded barber. For. A bird that scratches the earthly soil is banned from the sun-filled skies.

A body of ribs and reach. And. An edifice of bone and bracket. For. If the developments of steel and concrete make possible the construction of superstructures, it's the elevator that carries you away. Buildings up to four stories can be supported by walls. But. Your skyscraper requires a skeleton of steel. See. Lightning always strikes twice in your big city. Your Emerald City. And. There's hardly a place in the world where your pyrotechnic skyflowers cannot be seen. For. In the morning when the stars stop adorning, there are wars. And. When skyscrapers fall we shall have larks.

An instrument for carrying noise to a distance. Or. A mechanical device based on sound transportation. Or. An apparatus for conveying signals by means of electric speak. Or. A system of signaling by musical notes. As. A wind instrument like a foghorn used on ships for communicating. Loud harmonic notes. Like. The Marine Alarum. The Signal Trumpet. Pipes in which free tongues are acted upon by shallow breezes. Where. Air is admitted by means of a valve. By the needle of an electromagnet. Or. Air is released from a narrow orifice and divided. Upon the sharper edge. And. For. And. But. If the telephonic instrument can carry your voice over the diametrical distance of 7000 miles, I toss a pebble into this still pool. Then. I hear this tiny far-traveling tsunami die soundlessly in my mind. As there. So here. For. I hear your words. And. Your words have hammer. Or. Your voice has the madness of the metronome.

A tube for conveying the noise of ulterior voices. Among these are speaking tubes. For. We are, it seems, able to speak to the faraway places without any connection at all. As. Across the inner quadrangles of the cordiform building, for example. By means of a gutta-percha reflector.

A wonder of wonders. A lovers' tale. A stringed instrument. Or. A child's toy, consisting of two stretched membranes connected by a cord. Or. Connected by tension. Of. The past and its future. For. When I put my mouth to this membrane, you put your ear where? The game whose purpose is to efface the message as opposed to preserve it. As. My favorite flower is the rose. Then. Our Father has no nose.

A bell, a call, a dial. Drum, drum, drum. An extension, a booth, a box. But. If the telephonic instrument can carry your voice over the diametrical distance between us, my cord is off at the root. And. My voice can't worm. In other words, if the systemic soundness can be carried, I was born without discrimination or judgment. And. When the ring rings, there is someone on the telephoneforgiveme. Or. A manmade machine answers with a manmade voice. As. Please speak clearly. Please speak now. But. You're not on the telephone now.

Siphon

A tube bent so that one leg is longer than the other leg and used for drawing off liquids by. Atmospheric pressure. As. Which forces fluid up the shorter leg then over the bend. Or. A channel through which the passage of water becomes possible. Impossibly. As. A fire bucket. Or. A vessel made of tanned hides which carries the water to quench the fire raging amongst the Dwelling Houses. And. If the flow of fluid results from atmospheric pressure, you, again, put the tube in my mouth. You force the tube through the esophagus of my alimentary canal. And. Into my silver stomach. Then. You watch the heavy yellow liquor come up out from my inside. While I. Ask with unfinished fever. How can you do this to me?

You say. Fill a tube with fluid. Then. Pinch the two ends with your fingers. Put one end in the water bucket up above. Or. The exalted body on the bed. Then. Put the other end into the trenches. Unpinch your fingers and watch with your eyes as your insides flow through the tube and are carried out through your mouth. Your viscous soft sucking sounds. For. All the fervor of which you are capable is siphoned off into my army. And. I depend on the integration of the illicit functions that prostitution siphons off.

But. If the flow of fluid results from atmospheric pressure, it is also called an attracting engine. As. You ask. What do you expect from me? My guess is you are Birdsong. You sing these lullabies. And. I fall to sleep. For. The ebb and flow of springs sound like they are sung by your same siphon.

In one flock. As. Our sheep shall fear no wolf nor sudden storm. But go and come all safe in uniform. Or. Dress distinct in cut and color worn by a particular people. Recognized as properly belonging and peculiar. As. You are to consider what is to be furnished out of this last sum. A single suit. A separated garment. Customary dress characteristic of class. And. The person donning it. For. Of one character. Occurring in selfsameness. Exhibiting no difference or diversity. A franchise all federations follow. As. Hallowed be thy name. But. If the goal of timekeeping is to obtain a scale of uniform time, you fit snugly in your olive drab. Your field grey gabardine of grief. You march double time with other khaki cadavers. And make your death uniform to your life. While I remain your inanimate inmate. Dressed in zebra stripes perpendicular to those of your parallel prison. For. If things Past, Present, and to Come are strangely uniform and of one color, the symptoms of rupture are far.

From uni-. The earliest appearance of the element in English is naturally in words directly adopted from Latin. As. Unison. Universe. Unicorn. And -form. The nature, structure, or essence of a thing. Apart from content. The particular way that something appears. Apart from composition. And. A fixed mode of literary expression. As. Sestina. Sonnet. Ballad. And. Villanelle. But. If the goal of keeping is to obtain, you color your costume for the "home" and "away" games. And. Paris is the great uniform built. Thus. The stronglier situate.

The battledress of personnel. Medals of identification. Three corn e red hats. And. Infantry coats. Both visor and pompom. Both turn and fall collar. For. Bellbottoms and redcoats. Vied in green and white. And. If, the conclusion is that no time scale is uniform by measurement, this is of no practical consequence. For. I can only dream of wandering through your battlegreen fields. Donning the red and white roses of war.

A magic glass that forms the distant worlds. Or. A device for making faraway seem near. A photon bucket for collecting streams of discrete particles having zero mass, no electric charge, and infinitely long lifetimes. As. Above the height of mountains interposed, by what strange Parallax, or optic skill of vision, multiplied through air. Not exactly. Or. Never. But. If the instrument can render seeable the unseeable. Obvious the imperceptible. You put the balloon to your right eye and number the moons of Jupiter. You. Discover the rings of Saturn. Name the monstrous mountains of the lunar craters and witness black spots on the sun. While I, eclipsed by real proximity to your squinting left, wonder whether it be light or it be years that stand between.

Naturally, an objective lens set in a tube to focus the light from the astral plane. And. An eyepiece that grows the plane and brings the stars into view. Smaller hand scopes consist of two or more tubes made to slide within one another for convenience of packing in a narrow compass. Or. For tuning the zoom. But. There are reflectors and there are refractors. And. If the Kid's Kaleidoscope can offer the childish perspective, I wish I could shut up like the telescope. Fold my body in the palm of your lined hand. I demand my memory should use the telescope. For. I am trying hard to re-member myself. Or. I am trying hard to recall what it is to tell. As. The witness of space is one. The witness of me, on other hand.

To combine. To compress. To condense. To conflate and shorten by constriction. To force or drive into another. Something else. Said of railway carriages that collide. As. The express train ran into the locomotive thereby telescoping the baggage wagons. And. They telescoped like cars in railroad smashes. For. As you watch convexly the whirling oceans of your heavenly bodies, the proximate corpus collides. I see through this glass so darkly. For. It is I who am perpetually condemned to marry the mountains. Or. To marry the men who repeatedly die.

Mankind's third eye. Or. A system permitting visibility from an invisible position. A combination of a Telescope and a Camera Obscura. And. An apparatus used in a submarine for obtaining a view of objects above the water by a system of mirrors. A similar kind of tube-and-prism apparatus used on land. As in trench warfare. By which. A going to war. The action of war. A state of war. And. Military life or service. Always. But. If this third eye can bring to me a second sight, I call myself Commander and put my pupil to this bending lens. I survey the space above the break as if from a conning tower. Try to decipher your position. While you. Aboard the U-Boat of a different horizon. Evade my sight precisely.

The name of a Photographic object-glass. As. A Steinheil's periscope. And. Why the many styles of objectives? Orthoscope. Tachyscope. Euryscope. Periscope.

To peek around in a slanted fashion. To obtain a general comprehensive view. To perceive the panorama. As. When I periscope over this precipice. And. Where fishes' food is fed the shades who periscope through flowers to the sky.

One pipe encased in a protective pipe protruding upward from a submarine. As seen from above the sea, a tiny lighthouse. Or. A small pipe with an elbow joint. As. My ossified unstretched elbow. For. When the peri glides, my arm leaves a V-shaped foamy wake. A mark which betrays my presence. To the look out on your destroyer.

A plunging boat. Or. A vessel capable of propelling itself underwater. A craft of copper. A craft of rib. The Belly of the unsung whale. With a porthole permitting observation. Or. Lying beneath the surface. Lying at the bottom. As. Your laughter is profound. Or. A boat so designed. Like the old man of the sea's. See. You are submarine-minded. While I have a submarine mind. Or. I am robbed. By torpedoes. While moonlit spires and myriad lamps, shine like stars in the sublunar sky.

With enough air to keep four men and two candles for three hours. Burning. Or. Reaching knots for over an hour. As. Six months and two days. At slower speeds, a creeper. As. I am submersible. Or. I am the mermaid guiding the murmur.

Actively, to make oneself scarce in the presence of impending. Duty. Or. To slide, to drive, to throw it all under doom. A something said of something else. Or. A wood frame covered with leather. The oars extend through all the sides. Sealed with tight-fitted flaps.

A goatskin attached to a hull. As. Fill my skins with water. Then. Force me to dive and drive. An anti-ship war missile. As. The Guppy-hulled Nautilus. The teardrop Albacore. The doubled-up Narval and the interceptor Enterprise. Both the one-manned Turtle and the French Inflexible. The Mute is left to rot. Sinking at the moors. This is the Hunley. Attacking all harbors. Or. The Holland and the Sargo. The Gato and the Triton. While several musicians. An underwater rendition. For. Sing me an anthem. I am all thumbs stumbling. Or. I am stamping my memory. With your hand of sand and cave. This is the better evasion. You are a better equation. This is a book of lies. With open mouth and open eyes, up comes the submarine.

A circular basin of water. As. Into the theater, Atlas spouts. Or. A place constructed in the open air for the viewing of spectacles. Or. A segment of a circle. Excavated from a hillside. As. Shade above shade, a woody theater with the starriest view. And. An amphitheater. Or. A coliseum. A natural place for a play. As. House for comedy. House for tragedy. A picture palace for interludes. And. The alternative world lit by limelight. As. With scream and clap the theater quakes. But. If his head hangs low, the character is passive. If the light shines red, the character is possessed. I will be your Diana and haunt these fields. For. This theater of wood a fountain yields. Or. I am turning our Temple into a Theater. For. It's half past seven. And. I am standing spotlit on the platform of our play. Or. It's half past seven and I am standing spotlit in our black room. For. This is Theater of Others. Fit for a Theater of Gods. This is the Theater of Cruelty. And. I have chosen to communicate our storm. Or. The Theater of the Absurd. Mastered by Camus and acted out by myth.

Nuclear weapons for use within Europe. As. The United States has deployed a theater with delivery systems. Or. A region of the world in which a war is being fought. For. This is the Theater of War. So. Straighten your helmet and march robot-like into the show. And. This is the biggest battle the world will ever see. With woeful destiny and ditto misery. See. The audience is applauding. Or. The audience is gazing. With eyes cast down. On this. Our sad scene.

Actively, to contemplate. To go to the show. Theaterdom. The domain of things connected. Theaterless. Without entertainment. Theaterwise. In the manner. For. Rows and rows of people placed above one other. And. The drama itself. See. This is the tragedy where Time acts out his great fable. Or. This is the Theater Mundi. With dumb felicity and ditto misery. Thing displayed. Sight seen. A gazingstock. But. As you watch the show seated safely in the pit, the clown has cut off my hands again. The comedian has cut out my tongue. It's halfpast seven. And. I am standing.

Vacuum

Emptiness. Space unfilled. And. The area empty of air. Especially one from which air has been. Artificially withdrawn. And. The action of suction. This isolation. And. A void. A contained world in which the pressure is significantly lower than that of the atmosphere. But. While men have tried their best to achieve the World Devoid. Our Mother. The trunks of all substantive trees. It is as the saying goes. Nature abhors a vacuum. Succeeds in the deed of filling up unfilled fledglings. But. If the suction pump fails in the artificial effort, you endeavor to put your mouth to mine. Inhale the air from the space inside. And. Make my lungs two unfilled sacks. While I. Remembering the vacuum of your pupils, endeavor to fill myself up with our unrecorded past. For. Emptiness is not in the world. And. Larks from more adjacent parts do crowd.

Hear the pop of the broken bulb. Pull the cork from the bottle of burgundy. Push a pin in the blown balloon. For. The nightly noise of thunder. Lightning as it flashes. And. The air that collapses in and upon itself. Does clap. Who is my audience? For. This time I dispute against Democritus who believed the World was made by casual concourse. Of atoms in a giant vacuum.

No matter. It is the house that aches. For. You have forgotten the nests of birds. You must see the limbs of erupting trees. Or. You must see that I am. For. If the suction pump of your affection fails in the artificial effort, you must see that I matter.

With aspiration, a method of terminating pregnancy. With extractor, a cup-shaped appliance to assist a baby in its birth. With cleaner, a device for the removal of. Ashes to ashes. Mouth to mouth. Our past haunts. Empty rooms of. This is my body brick. And. If the suction pump of your affection fails in the artificial effort, you aspire to exhaust me. But. The void of me you so desire. Is impossible to produce. For. This time it is you, yourself, who fills the vessel. Of the matterless.

A frivolous fancy. And. A perverse presumption. A bizarre unreason on a zero topic held by persons of impressionistic tendencies. Or. A vision. A phantom. Fantastic. Also, a cross or an asterisk. As My head is full of windmills. Or. I have thoughts of you on my half-wit mind. For. A wind chime. A windfall. A wind instrument. As. An oboe. A trumpet. Or. A flute. More so. A mill in machinery blown by breezes that act upon its sails. And. A device used in flat districts for pumping still waters. But. If you become harnesser of Gods guilty of shaping the shapeless earth, I am harnessed only by the Goddess of Discordia. Good fortune is guiding my affairs. And. In the distance I see forty enormous Giants with whom I intend to do battle. For. It is a great service to God to remove so evil a breed from the rounder faces.

A fan, a blower, a draft, a leaf. A propellor, a ventilator, a thermantidote. As. A cooling medicine used to tame this heat. Or. A fan fixed in a window and incased in wet tatties. As. Screens of kuskus grass.

Generally, a style of bowling with overarm delivery. Necessarily, an airscrew. Literally. A toy consisting of cross-shaped cards fixed at the end of a stick. As. I going to the store and buy my child a windmill they sells made of paper. Or. To fly in the face of convention. As. She was a wild outward lass who enjoyed her youth with freedom and flung her shawl far over the windmill. Or. Over the rainbow. For. If you become the harnesser of the greater Gods, I stand every which way prepared to entertain fight. As. A windmill airplane flies over the English channel. And. I await the day your windmilly arms and angry eyes do fall.

X-ray

The beam of radiant energy whose essential nature is unknown. Or. Rays which produce fluorescence, phosphorescence, and other electrical effects, and which have a curative operation in certain skin diseases. Or. Radiation capable of passing through substances impervious to natural light. For. Substances normally opaque to light are rendered transparent by the unnatural system. And. Of affecting a sensitized plate. Thereby producing shadow-photographs of things enclosed within the skin. Like bones and bullets. Soft tissue and tumors. But. If the technology makes permissible the study of both skull and skeleton, you become the doctoral frontiersman. Radiologist. You use the unnatural science to turn me inside out. Penetrate my body and make the phosphorescent photographs of that beneath my flesh. While I. Lonely lying on this metal table. Attempt to deaden myself with more leaden dreams.

Energy produced by the deceleration of charged particles. Or. By electron transitions in atoms. This is of course in contrast to similar gamma rays which result from the radioactive decay of nuclei. But. If the technology communicates the secrets of the human hidden, you will see what I have said. Here, the bones are suffering from automatic erosion. Here, the bones are wrongly lucent. Here, the fusion of the synovial complexes. Or. The fusion of the joints. Here, my capacity for patience is quickly dwindling. For. Inside the waiting room of. This is my body blank. Time suffers the disease of. X marks the spot and. I am irradiating. For. What ever happened to that rain, Spain?

An examination in which an X-ray is taken. As. Ten patients were for immediate operation. A dozen or more were for X-ray. Several were likely to hemorrhage at any given moment. Or. Invisible rays now known to be a form of ether vibration with a wavelength shorter than short ultraviolet light. Or. To analyze. To break down. To dissolve. Or decompose. For. The X-ray has been instrumental in the study of crystals. And. When you render me transparent, you will see on your fluorescent screen. Here, in the penumbra of my ribcage. The shadows of my beating heart.

A continuous strand of twisted threads. Like wool or nylon. Used in weaving or knitting. Spindled fiber. As. Cotton. Silk. Or flax. An elaborate fiction or fairy. For. Tufts of crimson in cushions. Pearly strings on stairwells. These are the mingled yarns. Those are blended entrails. Or. One of the threads of which rope is composed. I ask you, How? You respond, Put the reel in a frame at the head. Then. Convey the register towards the thing. See the hook twists on the strand there. There where the process commences. But. Unless the whole thing is made right, this is just a dainty quay. With yarns about. Where eight women children spin worsted. So. Twist the knit around unfisted fingers in whatever shape of infinite. Then. Fold it over so it's an O. Wind as you normally would. But. I am another Penelope. They say the yarn I spun in your absence only filled Ithaca with Moths. Lies. Rumors. Proffered postcards. And boasts. These are my throwaway lines. Or. I am spinning garnet from birds. As. A vitreous mineral. Found in crystal. Projecting from pedicles of feldspar.

A thread of worsted in strands of rope made for the Royal Navy. For. Detecting embezzlement. Or. To trace the yarn to the yard.

You say, Nail the thing it in the middle of a scrap of oak. Or. Speak to me fair and canny. Weave, weaver. And. Ravel the hasp on the windle. I say, Tell me your story with a dash of snake. For. A weight suspended over the rolls produces the requisite tension. Or. I will cut the thread of life before the end of pain is carefully measured. But. You are a factoring fellow. Yarn is scaled in your weighhouse. While I am presenting a poem of sorts. Spun from reddened ruby. Or. I am biding my time with harlots. In the whitewashed rooms of Birdsville. For. This is the afghan pattern. Or. That is my body wrapped in yarn. And. After yarn is tarred, it is laid in the house to harden.

Naught or nil reckoned as a number. As. A five, with a zero and three to the left. Or. Absence of quantity considered a quantity. Or. The most practical invention of all. As. A sort of something that amounts to nothing. A kind of entity that connotes non-entity. A body. A nobody. The all-absorbing negation. And. The vanishing point. See. This is the beginning of it all. The zero hour. And. The attack is now due to begin. For. I hear a peal of laughter. And. In the Centigrade scales, the freezing point of water. In Fahrenheit, thirty-two degrees of frost. In games, the slot numbered zero of roulette. As. When the zero lands, the Bank itself takes half on all the chances. And. The French adopt it as the meridian that passes through the Observatory. But. If you take the conjunction, "I love," "He loved," "You may be loved," the word has *affix zero.* Or. With time adjuncts, omission of the preposition. As. Fifteen take zero as a plural.

In quantum physics, zero point is a form of motion in which there are no quasi-particles. As. In the zero night, you do not answer. At the zero of suffering, my mind is like an oak. Old and with brazen leaves. For. The point from which all reckoning. As. Ground Zero. Hurricane Zebra. These are the moments of truth. That is nothing at all. For. The hero of functions. A variable value by which all functions vanish. The power to shatter the frames of logic. This is the number without stone or bone.

A single-seated fighter used with great effect. Converted into kamikazes. As. Ditto, I zeroed in on the double downstairs. Or. You are my hero and I am your absolute nothing. For. Weightlessness. And. Zero gravity is the condition by which there is no apparent force. Or. In the zero atmosphere of America. You force me to forcelessness. Or. To set the sight. To concentrate. To get a closer view. As. With the camera angled widely on unsung shores. But. If the entropy of temperature corresponds to the order, it's Wittgenstein who zeroes in on language. Or. These are the secrets of the breakfast broadcast. And. Unless my Algebra deceives me, Unity divided by Zero always gives Infinity.

Sandy Florian was born in New York and raised in Latin America. She is of Colombian and Puerto Rican descent. She holds an MFA from Brown University's Creative Writing Program in Fiction. At Brown, she was the recipient of the Francis Mason Harris Award for best book-length manuscript written by a woman. She was also the recipient of the New Voices Sudden Fiction Prize in Cambridge. She lives in Denver where she is pursuing a PhD in English and Creative Writing. This is her first book.

Grateful acknowledgements are made to the following journals in which many of these poems were first published: *Kulture Vulture, Indiana Review, Bombay Gin, La Petite Zine, Shampoo Poetry, Washington Square Review, 14 Hills, elimae, New Orleans Review, eratio, Tarpaulin Sky, Gargoyle, 42 Opus, Copper Nickel, Word For/Word, Upstairs at Duroc, Segue, Versal, Prism Internationaland* and *The Encyclopedia Project.*

you are a little bit happier than i am by Tao Lin
Winner of the 2005 December Prize
ISBN: 0-9765692-3-X
ISBN: 978-0-9765692-3-7

Telescope by Sandy Florian
ISBN: 0-9765692-4-8
ISBN: 978-0-9765692-4-4

You go the words by Gunnar Björling,
translated by Frederik Hertzberg
Scandinavian Series #2
ISBN: 0-9765692-5-6
ISBN:: 978-0-9765692-5-1

The Edge of Europe by Pentti Saarikoski,
translated by Anselm Hollo
Scandinavian Series #3
ISBN: 0-9765692-6-4
ISBN: 978-0-9765692-6-8

lobo de labio by Laura Solórzano
translated by Jen Hofer
ISBN: 0-9765692-7-2
ISBN: 978-0-9765692-7-5

Remainland: Selected Poems of Aase Berg
Scandinavian Series #1
Johannes Göransson, Translator
ISBN 0-9765692-0-5

The Hounds of No by Lara Glenum
ISBN 0-97656592-1-3

My Kafka Century by Arielle Greenberg
ISBN 0-9765692-2-1

www.actionbooks.org